PAST PRESENT

PLACER COUNTY

T0274685

OPPOSITE: This 1916 photograph of Auburn's uptown Lincoln Street reflects the hustle-bustle activity of the day. Lincoln Street was originally called Railroad Street, as the railroad depot is at the end, just out of site. (Courtesy Placer County Museums.)

PAST PRESENT

PLACER COUNTY

Christina Richter

For my father, who was with me in spirit every step of the way.

Library of Congress Control Number: 2022950552

Published by Arcadia Publishing
Charleston, South Carolina

Printed in the United States of America

For all general information, please contact Arcadia Publishing:
Telephone 843-853-2070
Fax 843-853-0044
E-mail sales@arcadiapublishing.com
For customer service and orders:
Toll-Free 1-888-313-2665

Visit us on the Internet at www.arcadiapublishing.com

ON THE FRONT COVER: The city of Auburn was well established when the courthouse was completed in 1898. Today, the transportation corridor is seen where city streets and buildings once stood. (Past image, courtesy Placer County Museums; present image, courtesy Christina Richter.)

ON THE BACK COVER: Dutch Flat Independence Day celebrations have always been a popular event, as can be seen in this 1950s-era photograph. See page 73 for the present photograph and description of this historic hotel. (Courtesy Placer County Museums.)

CONTENTS

ACKNOWLEDGMENTS

A publication such as this takes a great deal of support from many kindred spirits. My family was my rock. My daughters Audrey and Anna and most especially my husband, Mark, gave me their encouragement, coffee, and shoulder rubs as needed.

The wonderful people at the Placer County Water Agency, specifically Brie Anne Coleman and Ed Horton, made the dream of including a chapter about the county's water history possible. Huge thanks to Sean Bigley at the City of Roseville for the connection.

My first successful Auburn photo shoot was thanks to the 2020 Historian of the Year, Dave Allen. Former Auburn mayor and city council member Mike Holmes was also a great support. I am grateful to Barbara Leak of the Loomis Historical Society. Barbara is a blessing to our county as her wealth of knowledge and understanding of the area is unparalleled. Rocklin Historical Society's David Baker and Jim Carlson readily shared their insights and knowledge. The Colfax Historical Society is truly an asset to its community, and Roger Staab and Nancy Hageman lead the effort. Cliff Kennedy helped in my quest for Penryn history, and Mike Monahan was indispensable in sharing Newcastle history. It was my honor to work with each of these pros.

It was also my honor to work with Elizabeth Jensen, Mary Dillingham, Bill Clinton, and Shirley Russell of the Lincoln Historical Society; Sarah and Thom Fugate of the Golden Drift Historical Society; and Sandy and Troy Simester of the Forest Hill Divide Historical Society.

Special thanks to the Roseville City Library for a couple of hard-to-find photographs and to Roseville city manager Dominick Casey for sharing Roseville's recognized historic buildings with me early on in this project. Also huge thanks to supervisor Bonnie Gore and past mayor Susan Rohan for their support and insight.

The staff at the Placer County Archives was invaluable. Kelsey Monahan was exceptionally wonderful, allowing me to spend hours doing research, answering my many questions, and providing the majority of past photographs in this book.

The Placer County Archives history collection is extensive thanks to the generosity of individuals and organizations who have understood the importance of sharing historical research and photographs through the years. Thank you, especially, for the decades of important work that the Placer County Historical Society has provided.

Finally, a huge thank-you to local historian Rodi Lee. Her edits and keen insight provided a gentle guiding light.

Unless otherwise noted, all past images appear courtesy of Placer County Museums.

Unless otherwise noted, all present images were taken by the author, Christina Richter.

INTRODUCTION

Placer County is distinctive both in topography and history. It covers 1,500 square miles of land and stretches about 65 miles end to end. Within the county, the Sierra Nevada reaches 8,683 feet, and the valley lowlands drop to nearly sea level. Oftentimes, snow glistens on the mountains year-round.

The earliest people living here created trade-route pathways that were used for thousands of years. In the 19th century, these same pathways were discovered by hunters, fur trappers, and early California settlers. Those routes later served as trails for immigrant wagon trains and as a road map for the gold rush–era traveler.

Gold was discovered in nearby Coloma in January 1848, and in May of that same year nuggets were unearthed in the area now known as Auburn in Placer County. In December 1848, President Polk announced that he could confirm the rumors of an abundant amount of gold in California. With this announcement, the Gold Rush of 1849 was officially begun.

Along with gold, water also played a large part in Placer County history. It was the best and most effective way to separate gold from rock, so industrious miners set about the arduous task of bringing water to their claims. As a result, miles of "simple but elegant" water ditches and canals were created.

By the end of the 1850s, ranching, farming, and sawmills began to replace gold mining as the county's economic engine. Plentiful water enabled productive sawmills. Water combined with rich soil provided the catalyst for extensive operations of acres of farms and ranchland. The most difficult aspect of getting these rich resources to market was the lack of efficient transportation.

Once the transcontinental railroad was completed in 1869, its impact on Placer County was immeasurable. The railroad connected significant trading posts and towns, making import and export almost easy compared to the county's beginning days.

As wilderness turned into civilization, tents and cabins were replaced with more solid structures. Through time, those structures were rebuilt with longevity in mind.

Those buildings and their times provide an indelible memory as we peruse the photographs of their past. These images offer highlights of a county that grew from the wealth of the Gold Rush, the innovation of the railroad, and the strength and fortitude of its people.

THE COUNTY SEAT

Local resources were used to build the stately, three-story, Classic Revival Auburn courthouse structure, completed in 1898. Granite from Rocklin and bricks and terra-cotta trim from Gladding McBean in Lincoln are a beautiful part of this building. It is seen here with the old, original 1853 courthouse and 1856 brick jailhouse still on site.

Commercial Street includes some of the earliest structures in Auburn and is often considered the oldest street in the city. Today, the 1860 Native Sons of the Golden West building anchors the street at the top, and the "Round Corner" anchors the street at the bottom. There have been many businesses in the walls of these venerable old structures, and plaques on each of the buildings tell the story of their past.

The ornate Orleans Hotel and surrounding buildings were demolished with the establishment of the transportation corridor. It is not exactly certain when the site became a hotel, but it is known that the first building burned in the fire of 1855. The structure was rebuilt but burned again in 1863. Once again rebuilt and documented as a hotel, it was purchased in 1881 and remodeled. The hotel's demolition in 1959 became the spark for a citizen's movement to save Auburn's historic structures.

The Masonic Lodge in Auburn is located at 948 Lincoln Way and is listed in the National Register of Historic Places. It began as a one-story building that housed a department store in 1906. The second story was added and dedicated in April 1916 as meeting space for the local Masonic fraternity. The facade is made of terra-cotta from the Gladding McBean plant in Lincoln. Today, the structure is a prominent landmark on the Central Square in Auburn.

Also known as "The Old Auburn Library," the Auburn Carnegie Library was dedicated in May 1909 and is located at 175 Almond Street. One of three Carnegie libraries in Placer County, it was built with assistance from a grant from the Andrew Carnegie Foundation. It operated as part of the library system until 1968 and was placed in the National Register of Historic Places in March 2011. Today, the city-owned vacant building awaits a new tenant.

Originally, the site of the Auburn Promenade was a fruit preserving building. It was remodeled and opened as the Putnam hotel in 1880. A fire in 1881 destroyed the structure, but it was immediately rebuilt. The structure went through a series of hotel owners before it burned again in 1912, then became the Auburn Hotel in 1914. The hotel was renovated in the late 1980s into retail shops and is now known as the Auburn Promenade.

LINCOLN WAY--1930's

Auburn Calif.

THE COUNTY SEAT

The stately Mission-style Tahoe Club building on High Street in Auburn was completed in 1914. It was designed by San Francisco architect Frank S. Holland. The all-male club was founded in 1909 and at the time of the building's dedication had a membership list of 100 people. In this 1916 photograph, the Episcopal church can be seen at the end of the street. The view is looking south from High and East Placer Streets.

This 1913 building at 874 Lincoln Way is in the National Register of Historic Places and continues to serve its original purpose as a bank. It was designed by San Francisco architect Charles Kaiser Sumner with granite steps, bronze-finished lamps, and gold leaf decorated friezes. It was considered to house a strong and influential financial institution that proudly served the citizens of Placer County. This Auburn building is still kept in a beautiful state.

THE COUNTY SEAT

The esteemed building at 1103 High Street in Auburn was placed in the National Register of Historic Places in 2012. It was designed by the first state architect of California, George Clinton Sellon, and built in 1935. It also holds the distinction as being a Works Progress Administration (WPA) project and is considered "modern" architecture. Today, it houses the Placer County Visitor's Bureau and Auburn Chamber of Commerce.

The World War II DeWitt hospital was designed as a "Type-A" style and was one of only 16 of its kind in the country. It officially opened on February 26, 1944. After the war was over, the US Army closed the hospital on December 31, 1945. It was then purchased by the state to serve as a mental institution and was known as the DeWitt State Hospital for 25 years. Today, the historic facility is part of the Placer County government center.

Administration Bldg. and Officer's Quarters
De Witt General Hospital _ Auburn, Calif.

THE COUNTY SEAT

FREEMAN HOTEL. AUBURN. BUILT 1866

The original Freeman Hotel was erected in 1866, burned down, then rebuilt in 1868. In 1892, a large spring dance floor was added outside. This photograph shows the three-story annex added beside the original building. Its close location to the railroad depot, coupled with its fine and detailed amenities, enabled the hotel to cater to VIPs traveling into town. The site also boasted stables and tennis courts. It was torn down in 1970 and replaced with the current strip mall.

The rededication of the uptown Auburn Post Office occurred in 1964. When the building was completed in 1939, it was celebrated as one of the most contemporary structures in Auburn. It was built under the secretary of the treasury with supervising architect Louis A. Simon. This 1964 group gathering includes May Perry, the original curator of the Placer County Museums. Official mail service began in Auburn in 1849.

THE COUNTY SEAT

In 1888, a local Auburn newspaper announced that "a fine two-story house on the hill south of town was being built by E.C. Snowden." It went on to say that "Snowden will commence the erection of a $2,500 house on his lot back of Main Street and it is hoped that a new street will soon be opened on the ridge from Mr. Snowden's lot to the Racetrack Road." Today, the beautifully located hillside home serves as a boutique hotel.

The citizens of Auburn were delighted to open their opera house in November 1891. The beautiful building was a hub of activity and served as the town's entertainment center for several decades. As time went on, its popularity was replaced with other venues. It burned down in 1957 and was not replaced. The building once stood at the intersection of Lincoln Way and High and Lewis Streets in the center of the Central Square.

THE VILLAGE THAT BECAME A CITY

Roseville's first store was opened by William Alexander Thomas in 1865 at the corner of Lincoln and (old) Atlantic Streets. Thomas previously owned the 15-Mile House, which serviced the teaming and stagecoach trades. With changing times, Thomas opened a new modern store with a train town focus. This building was moved in 1910, and today, railroad tracks are in its place.

The Vernon Street Presbyterian Church was the second church to be built in Roseville and was completed in 1883. In 1910, the structure was pressed into a new use as Roseville's first permanent city hall. The building received an updated facade in 1916, and in 1936, it was part of WPA improvements during the Great Depression. The historic structure was razed in 2015 to construct the present four-story, 82,000-square-foot office building.

Roseville grew up on both sides of the railroad tracks and in the early days this separation caused great traffic congestion. In June 1910, voters approved $1,500 for a wooden bridge to span the railroad tracks to connect Lincoln and Sierra Streets. The original bridge was replaced in 1929 with a safer concrete structure but still maintained its "crooked" aspect, and a rainbow arch was added. The bridge looks as it did in 1929 and remains a busy thoroughfare.

The iconic Roseville Bank of Italy office building is at the intersection of Lincoln and Church Streets. The site was developed in 1907 for the Roseville Banking and Trust Co. The Bank of Italy became the new owners in 1920, then in 1927, the building was replaced with a Bank of America structure. This site operated continuously as a bank until 1966. The *Roseville Press Tribune* occupied the building from 1966 to 1976. Today, Old Town Roseville patrons enjoy this beautiful landmark.

THE VILLAGE THAT BECAME A CITY

HOTEL BARKER—Roseville, Cal.!!!!

When the Barker Hotel was built in 1911 at the corner of Lincoln and Atlantic Streets, Roseville had begun a significant growth period. In less than three years the town saw 110 new buildings. As the town grew, Roseville housed many traveling railroad workers and others with related business. The in-demand Barker Hotel served their needs perfectly as it was situated close to the railroad depot and the town. The popular Boxing Donkey restaurant is housed here today.

The McRae Opera House was completed in October 1908 and opened with great ceremony. No town was considered proper without an opera house, and this building answered the need. Its upper level was a fine hall used for entertainment. A market and office space occupied the street level. It was an important community destination point for decades. Today, the Opera House Bar is on the first floor, and the recently renovated upper level serves as an event venue.

THE VILLAGE THAT BECAME A CITY

Education was important to the early citizens of Roseville. Originally, high school classes were held in a repurposed railroad building, on the second floor, with the first floor housing the Golden Eagle Saloon. The new Roseville High School was completed in December 1915. Due to new California earthquake standards, the original school was replaced in 1970. It still operates as a high school, and it is likely the site will always be "The High School On The Hill."

Roseville was established at the junction of the Central Pacific and California Central Railroads in 1864 with a temporary depot built at this time. A permanent building was erected in 1874. A new depot was built in 1907 that operated until 1972, when it was closed and passenger services were discontinued. It was later razed. In 1987, passenger traffic was restored, and a new railroad depot opened in 1994. Its design pays homage to Southern Pacific railroad stations from the early 20th century.

THE VILLAGE THAT BECAME A CITY

William Haman built this home in 1909 at the corner of Oak and Taylor Streets, just a few blocks from his workplace. Haman was brought to Roseville to manage the Placer County Winery. He would become one of Roseville's prominent citizens, serving many community roles. Haman died in 1931, and his wife, Alice, resided in the home until her death. Alice also had an affinity for exotic cats. The privately owned historic home currently sits vacant and in disrepair. (Courtesy City of Roseville Library, Local History Collection.)

ROSEVILLE, CALIF.   EASTMAN'S STUDIO   B-8357

In 1954, the movie *The Glenn Miller Story* with James Stewart was released and was shown in the theater at the Roseville Masonic Temple building on Vernon Street. By 1954, Roseville was the largest populated city in Placer County, and Vernon Street served as its major shopping area. The 1926 Masonic Temple is the oldest structure on Vernon Street and has served continuously as a theater on the first floor with the Masons on the upper two stories.

THE VILLAGE THAT BECAME A CITY

The now city-owned post office at 330 Vernon Street in Roseville is seen here just after it was built in 1935 as part of the WPA effort during the Great Depression. The building has undergone several renovations, but the original interior is largely the same. It once housed commissioned Depression-era art by Zygmund Sazevich entitled *The Letter*. Sen. Harold "Bizz" Johnson also had an office here. The fate of this historic site is undetermined at this time.

From 1883 to 1929, the Andrew Carnegie Foundation donated $55 million to help build over 2,500 libraries worldwide. Three of those libraries were built in Placer County, with the Roseville Carnegie Library being completed in October 1912. In 1979, its replacement, a new main library on Taylor Street, was built. Much discussion ensued regarding the building's future. Finally on October 12, 1988, the newly renovated city building was opened as a local history museum and children's day care center.

THE VILLAGE THAT BECAME A CITY

Roseville can attribute most of its early growth to the railroad. An artificial ice-making plant was built in 1908, and in 1913, the Pacific Fruit Express Company invested $75,000 to expand its ice-making facility from 15,000 to 30,000 tons. For decades the Pacific Fruit Express refrigerator cars were a common site on local railroad tracks. The ice plant was eventually replaced with modern technology and was razed in 1974. Today, the railroad cars going through Roseville reflect a different era.

The building at 103 Lincoln Street has served as one of the longest, continually operating funeral businesses in Placer County. It was built in 1932 as a funeral parlor to serve the established Broyer family business. To ease costs, devoted citizens pitched in to help with its construction. When finished, it was reported as a "fireproof" Spanish architecture structure with a cost of just over $15,000. Today, it continues to be family operated by Cochrane & Wagemann Funeral Directors. (Courtesy City of Roseville Library, Local History Collection.)

WORLD FAMOUS FOR CLAY

Gladding McBean was established in Lincoln after potter's clay was discovered in 1875. This photograph shows the 1890 interior yard with the rail line going into the clay factory. Wood was stacked close to the tracks ready to be used as fuel for the train and to fire pottery kilns. Clay pipe is also stacked and ready to be shipped. (Courtesy Lincoln Area Archives Museum.)

The 1921 Lincoln Civic Auditorium is a Spanish Colonial Revival structure and is a beautiful example of Gladding McBean ornamentation. The lower arches and windows are surrounded by a decorative rope design in glazed terra-cotta, and the upper facade boasts a unique diagonal brick inlay with terra-cotta medallions and parapet scrolls. The auditorium was used for plays, dances, concerts, and other community functions. Today, the interior has been remodeled but the exterior remains almost exactly the same. (Past image, courtesy Lincoln Area Archives Museum.)

WORLD FAMOUS FOR CLAY

The Lincoln Carnegie Library at the corner of Fifth and F Streets was completed in 1909. The Carnegie Foundation donated $6,000 in grant funding, and the town raised an additional $3,000. Gladding McBean also donated the bricks used for the structure. The lamppost added in front was used by many cities that were building a Carnegie Library as it was thought to be a symbol of enlightenment. Today, the city-owned building is not in use as a public facility. (Past image, courtesy Lincoln Area Archives Museum.)

The Lincoln Funeral Home was built in 1930 by Milton W. Hogle. In 1909, Hogle had acquired Ed Hill's mortuary business (established 1889). W.F. Farnsworth purchased the building in 1939 and operated it as a funeral and ambulance service until 1964. It continued as a funeral home and is presently owned by the Dignity Memorial Corporation. The early photograph was taken in the summer of 1939. This building very likely houses the longest, continually operating funeral home in the county. (Past image, courtesy Shirley Russell.)

WORLD FAMOUS FOR CLAY

The Methodist church building at Sixth and I Streets is the oldest standing church in Lincoln. Its cornerstone was laid in 1890, and construction began in June. The original steeple was nearly twice as tall as it is today, but it was shortened after strong winds took it down twice. Inside are 37 unique stained-glass windows with many that highlight ministers and missionaries who traveled west. The building continues to serve as a church. (Past image, courtesy Lincoln Area Archives Museum.)

The original one-room Fruitvale Schoolhouse in rural Lincoln began serving students in 1889. A second classroom was added in 1923. The school continued for decades but necessarily stopped in 1946. The times surrounding World War II invoked school changes, and from 1946 to 1970, it served as a community center and polling place. An extensive restoration campaign in 2001 was recognized with the Governor's Historic Award. Today, the building serves as a museum, a living history program space, and community rental property.

This beautiful home in old town Lincoln was built in 1913 by the Gladding family as a wedding present for the oldest grandson of the founder, Charles Gladding. It is a Frank Lloyd Wright design called the Prairie Home. Originally, it was built as part of the Gladding compound, which included two houses, a carriage barn, a swimming pool, a rose garden, and tennis court. The home is now in the Keller family, who lovingly care for it today. (Past image, courtesy Lincoln Area Archives Museum.)

This stretch of buildings on Fifth Street in Lincoln originally housed a livery stable. The Burdge Hotel was first constructed in 1861 and the Odd Fellows building in 1864. The Independent Order of Odd Fellows (IOOF) building was expanded to its current configuration in 1905. The hotel site operated from 1861 to 1940, housing three iterations of the Burge Hotel. In 1940, the hotel was torn down to make way for a gas station. The IOOF building today houses a popular restaurant and event center. (Past image, courtesy Lincoln Area Archives Museum.)

WORLD FAMOUS FOR CLAY

TRAINS AND FRUIT

Colfax and Loomis grew up as both fruit and train towns. The Central Pacific Railroad reached Loomis in 1864 and Colfax in 1865. Colfax became the distribution point for freight hauling to nearby towns. Production of fruit expansion in the foothills contributed heavily to the local economies. This photograph shows the 1912 Colfax railroad depot. (Courtesy Pacific Railroad Historical Society.)

The Colfax Hotel, originally known as the Gillen Hotel, had its grand opening on March 12, 1903. Colfax, being on the Southern Pacific Railroad line as well as the Nevada County Narrow Gauge Railroad line, had a large number of travelers as a result of the volume of both freight and passenger business flowing through town. The hotel originally had 56 rooms and a dining room that seated 100 people. The building is currently under renovation. (Past image, courtesy Colfax Historical Society.)

TRAINS AND FRUIT

This c. 1935 photograph of the Kaufman Brothers Colfax Garage is a great glimpse into the filling stations and garages of yesteryear. The structure, originally erected in 1920, is claimed to be the oldest building in Colfax operating continuously as an automobile body shop. The current building has a modified facade and has been expanded. It remains a popular Colfax destination for auto work. (Past image, courtesy Colfax Historical Society.)

The Stagi Brothers Bakery first opened in 1907 on Depot Street, at the end of Main Street, in Colfax. The bakery was strategically built across from the original depot and railroad tracks to attract travelers and was a popular place for locals as well. The new building is nearly identical to the original and currently houses a pharmacy and nail salon. The historic and charming character of Colfax is represented in this building. (Past image, courtesy Colfax Historical Society.)

A fire destroyed the earlier two-story building on this site in October 1933. The Lobner Block was then built shortly after the fire as a single-story structure, and it housed the popular corner establishment called the Donner Club. In 1978, the entire building was modified significantly to look like the earlier structure on this site. A restaurant now occupies the prior Donner Club section. (Past image, courtesy Colfax Historical Society.)

The Colfax Market is thought to be the oldest retail business site in the area, having been originally built in 1865. In 1870, Hayford Hines and Company established a general merchandise store here. The structure burned in the 1931 fire and was rebuilt. Through the years, it has always served as a general merchandise store. The earlier photograph was taken around 1926. (Past image, courtesy Colfax Historical Society.)

TRAINS AND FRUIT

In 1875, Colfax was one of the leading towns of the county with an estimated population of 1,000. The Colfax Grammar School was built to meet the town's demand for education and accommodated children up to the eighth grade. The beautiful c. 1890 building was erected in the Carpenters Gothic style. It burned down in 1912. A new school was built in its place in 1938 as an Art Deco–style WPA project. Today, the building serves as the Sierra Vista Community Center. (Past image, courtesy Colfax Historical Society.)

The Loomis Fruit Growers Association (LFGA) was the last fruit shed operating in Placer County, closing its doors in May 2001. The company began in 1901, just two years after Loomis built its first fruit house in 1889. LFGA was the first to build a modern, highly mechanized packinghouse in 1926. At its peak in the 1930s and 1940s, there were 22 fruit sheds in Placer County. The old LFGA structure is part of the present-day High Hand Nursery building.

The Central Pacific Railroad reached this area in 1864 and would play a vital role in Placer County's developing economy. In 1910, the Southern Pacific Railroad built a new train depot in Loomis to accommodate the booming fruit growing and shipping center. Fruit sheds once lined the railroad tracks as freight trains would load up with produce and passengers. Thousands of packed fruit boxes were shipped east for auction. Today, the depot has been refurbished and serves as a community center.

Downtown Loomis was devastated in the 1915 fire, but the Cook and Co. store building survived. The brick structure was completed in 1912, and its wagons are seen here ready to deliver groceries and goods to local citizens. In the early photograph, the Turner stable and May's Loomis Livery Stable are also seen. Today, the site houses a new building with Ace Backyard as its tenant.

COOK & CO., STORE, LOOMIS, CALIF. 1912

Main Street in Loomis has changed through the years, but it still remains a very busy place. The 1906 photograph, with a Thomas Flyer car, shows perspective of the number of businesses. The street housed a grocery and drugstore, bank, post office, barbershop, and a shed for horses from the livery stable. Also on the street are an icehouse, butcher shop, saloon, and lodge hall. At the far end were the blacksmith shop and fruit sheds.

DRUG STORE LOOMIS

The Pendleton family's Thomas Flyer car, reported to be the first car in Loomis, is shown here in 1906 in front of the Loomis Drug Co. Owner Al Pendleton had an operating mine as well as productive orchards. Al is the driver; his son Norman and pharmacist Bill Hewes are the passengers. Next door are the barbershop and Wells Fargo bank businesses. The Thomas Flyer car was made famous by its record-setting 48-day crossing of the United States.

ORIGINAL ROUNDHOUSE PLACE

Rocklin Cal.   F.A.Lewis.

The Rocklin Roundhouse opened in May 1867 with 25 engine stalls, a turntable, and a very large woodshed. Its location was at the intersection of Front Street and what is now Rocklin Road. The facility burned in both 1869 and 1873 and was rebuilt each time. The roundhouse operation was relocated permanently to Roseville in 1908; it employed 300 people prior to its move. (Courtesy Rocklin Historical Society.)

The Central Pacific Railroad reached Rocklin from Sacramento in May 1864, and passenger service began almost immediately. Rocklin's first depot was possibly a railcar on a side track near the current depot. A permanent rail station was built in 1867; the depot in the early photograph is seen as it was in 1906. The existing depot, built in 2007, is home to the Rocklin Chamber of Commerce and bears a plaque of the 1864 local train schedule. (Past image, courtesy Rocklin Historical Society.)

ORIGINAL ROUNDHOUSE PLACE

Front Street in 1913 shows a thriving town with retail and business buildings. Rocklin was in a robust economy as there were 27 quarries in operation, employing 500–600 men. The stone structure, known as the Barudoni building, was erected in 1905 as a meat market downstairs and doctor's office upstairs. In 1914, a significant fire destroyed many of these buildings but left the stone Barudoni structure intact. Today, Front Street houses offices, and the Barudoni building is a popular winery. (Past image, courtesy Rocklin Historical Society)

The Finnish Temperance Hall on Rocklin Road can be seen in this view looking south from Grove Street. The past photograph depicts typical residential areas of early Rocklin, with well-kept homes, white picket fences, and pathways located above the dirt road. Citizens gathered at the beautiful 1905 Finn Hall building for many of Rocklin's social functions. The City of Rocklin purchased the building in 1962 to ensure its preservation. (Past image, courtesy Rocklin Historical Society.)

ORIGINAL ROUNDHOUSE PLACE

The elegant Finnish Temperance Hall is shown as it looked in 1910. The Rocklin Historical Society's monument states: "This Hall Dedicated to: The People From Finland Who Immigrated To Rocklin, The Finnish Temperance Society Who Built The Hall in 1905, The United Finnish Kaleva Brothers And Sisters Lodge No. 5 Of Rocklin California." Its renovation was completed in 1989. Finn Hall has been the home of theater programs since 1994. Today, the year-round Rocklin Community Theater group rehearses and performs here. (Past image, courtesy Rocklin Historical Society.)

The Whitney Oaks mansion, also known as The Oaks, was once part of Joel Parker Whitney's 20,000-acre Spring Valley Ranch. In the mid-1880s, the wealthy Whitney built a proper English baronial estate for his extended family, and in 1884, his great manor house was completed. Whitney and his immediate family thrived here for 29 years. The home was torn down in 1951 as the tax burden for the owners was too heavy. Today, the site is a developed neighborhood. (Past image, courtesy Rocklin Historical Society.)

At the turn of the 20th century, Railroad Avenue in Rocklin was bustling with business and commerce buildings. Both the J.C. Ford and P.J. Freeman establishments offered a wide variety of services, including furniture sales, stoves, and general merchandise. Freeman was also an undertaker and operated his business here. All that remains of this once busy place are foundations that can be observed under a warehouse building and throughout the block. (Past image, courtesy Rocklin Historical Society.)

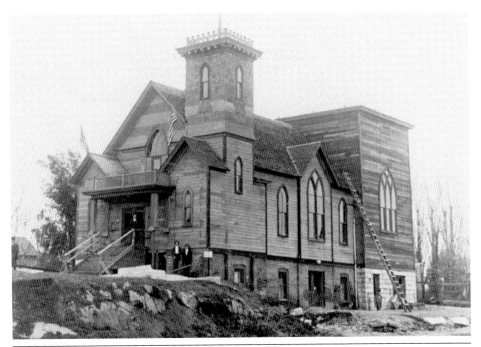

The 1893 Methodist church at the corner of San Francisco and Rocklin Roads was repurposed in 1914 as a Labor Temple for organized labor efforts in Rocklin. An addition that included a large stage was built onto the back of the building, making the space suitable for civic and social functions. Union demand discussions for the Granite Strike of June 1915–January 1916 were held here. The well-used structure was torn down in the early 1930s. (Past image, courtesy Rocklin Historical Society.)

ORIGINAL ROUNDHOUSE PLACE

CHAPTER

FOOTHILL
COMMUNITIES

This c. 1905 Newcastle square scene illustrates the activity of a thriving foothill town. For most of its early history, Newcastle was a major fruit-growing and shipping center. The Pomona Hotel is pictured in the left rear of the photograph, across from Fruit House Row. Dozens of farmers with produce-loaded wagons await their turn to unload their goods for shipping.

Known as Depot Hill in Dutch Flat, in 1882 the Faller home, a saloon, and railroad depot stood at this site. A separate depot structure was built later. The gentleman in the photograph is Ed Duffy. Duffy spoke fluent Chinese and often acted as an interpreter for the town's Chinese citizens. Dutch Flat boasted more than 2,000 Chinese residents between 1850 and 1860. Today, the site is nearly vacant with little evidence of its past.

The Dutch Flat Methodist Episcopal Church was constructed in 1859 under the auspices of the Methodist Conference. The timbers used were cut from the hillside and hewn by hand, the pews are from New England, and the cupola was added in 1866. In 1987, the church underwent a major remodeling effort paid for by friends in the community and members of the church. A meeting hall was added in 1996. Today, the structure is designated as a historic landmark.

The Dutch Flat schoolhouse sits on the site of an 1851 cabin that housed the first settlers in the area, the Dornenbach family. In 1859, the first school was built here as a single-story structure. The second schoolhouse was then constructed in 1875 as a two-story building. The present building, the third schoolhouse, was erected in 1898 after an arsonist fire burned the previous school to the ground. A school operated here until 1962; today, the building serves as a community center.

The first home on this Fifth Avenue property has an unusual past. The original owner, M.S. Gardiner, owned the Dutch Flat Water Company in partnership with E.L. Bradley. This company supplied water for the local hydraulic mining operations. It was purchased by a Mr. Berg in 1920, and rumors indicated that the new owner had instituted gambling in his house. The home burned under mysterious circumstances in 1921. The current structure is home to Dutch Flat residents.

The Dutch Flat Masonic Lodge and Independent Order of Odd Fellows (IOOF) structures were built within five years of each other—Masonic Lodge in 1856 and the IOOF in either 1859 or 1860. Both were constructed as single-story buildings to house businesses. In the 1860s, the Masons added a second story, and the Odd Fellows added another floor in 1873. The IOOF building continues to serve its original purpose, the Masonic Hall building is now privately owned.

The original Dutch Flat Hotel was built in 1852 as a long, narrow, two-story structure. It was expanded in 1868, and a third story was added in 1875. In its heyday, the hotel had 52 guest rooms, a large dining room, and a popular saloon. Its current configuration was created in a 1920 remodel. The hotel served as a private residence from 1941 to 2004. Once again remodeled, today it continues as one of the oldest operating hotels in California.

An iteration of the Forest House in Foresthill has been part of this community almost continuously since the beginning days. The original Forest House was built in 1850 as a trading post on the road leading to the mines in the upper divide. In total there have been four Forest House hotels. The present structure was built in 1947 and is the fourth Forest House, as the first three burned down. Today, it continues as a hotel and event center.

Foresthill attracts travelers to its area for various reasons. The Tevis Cup, which goes through Foresthill, is an endurance horseback ride that includes 100 miles of the Western States Trail, of which 14 miles are in the National Register of Historic Places. The event has run annually since 1955. Today, it is not unusual to see a tourist van parked in front of the Forest House hotel as it offers travelers a glimpse of the historic area.

The Foresthill St. Patrick Catholic Church was originally established in 1861. An unusually heavy snowfall in 1885 caused the structure to collapse. The church was then rebuilt closer to town in 1888. That building was destroyed by fire in 1952. The top of the stone monument on the site can be seen today behind the now residential property fence. The monument once housed the church bell, which has recently been relocated to the Foresthill cemetery.

MAIN STREET FOREST HILL
BUSINESS BLOCK   CALIF.

The upper end of Main Street houses the Foresthill business block. In 1859, the post office was transferred from the defunct gold mining town of Bath to Foresthill. It was housed here in the general store and was the first community post office. Mail was taken by stagecoach to Foresthill from Auburn and Colfax. The 1861 Odd Fellows building once had an upper balcony. The corner building is now a restaurant. There are several small businesses in the block today.

By 1880, Foresthill was one of the largest towns in Placer County. Needing to accommodate the many travelers to the area, the lovely two-story Central Hotel and Bar was built. It was owned by W. Rea and is often referred to as the Rea Hotel. The building was destroyed by fire in 1933 and was never rebuilt. The site is now a vacant lot, and the community Christmas tree is on display here each year.

The Foresthill School District was organized in 1858. Perhaps Foresthill's most famous event occurred on August 19, 1859, when Col. Edward Dickerson Baker made a political speech against slavery in front of the schoolhouse on Main Street to 600–700 town residents. The original Foresthill School was eventually abandoned for a larger structure and was repurposed as part of the building of three other structures.

OLD FOREST HILL SCHOOL

The Foresthill DeMaria family home has a storied past. The property was purchased by the DeMaria family in 1886 for $700, and the home was completed about 1890. Part of the home is where the original Spring Garden Post Office was housed; Clement DeMaria was postmaster. Clement was the great- grandfather of the present-day owner. The home fell out of the family around 1965, but it was purchased by Annie DeMaria-Norris and her husband in July 2017 and restored to its present grandeur. (Past image, courtesy Annie De-Maria-Norris.)

The elegant Newcastle Hotel opened in 1901. It was intentionally built near the railroad depot and was considered to be the best, well-furnished hotel in Placer County. It had 67 rooms with a bath on each floor. In the early 1900s, Newcastle was booming with 10 fraternal societies and two public halls supporting the community. The hotel burned on July 28, 1920. Today, the site is home to a local business.

VIEW IN BUSINESS SECTION BEFORE THE BIG FIRE

Fruit sheds were built along Newcastle's railroad tracks so that produce could be easily delivered and then shipped. In 1894, a record 20-million-plus pounds of fruit was shipped. Fire ravaged the buildings in 1900, then again in 1922. The business buildings in this past photograph were constructed adjacent to the fruit sheds and supported the lucrative business with retail and services. A small town plaza named Marshall Square was dedicated in July 1987 and remains a nod to modern-day Newcastle.

FOOTHILL COMMUNITIES

The Placer Buddhist Church community in Penryn was founded in 1902 with approximately 50 members. A proper church was built in 1920 and also included parsonage and social hall buildings. It was considered the heart and soul of the community and served as a religious center for the area's Buddhists. The church relocated to a new facility in 1963. The 1920 building now serves as the Foursquare Church as part of the Penryn Faith Center.

With the establishment of his granite quarry in 1864, Griffith Griffith began today's Penryn; originally known as Penrhyn from his Welsh roots. Griffith constructed this two-story stone building in 1878, and it is considered an example of the California Victorian Gothic style. Since 1880, the top floor of the building has been utilized by the Masonic Order. Today, it houses the Penrhyn Gold Hill Lodge No. 32 and Penrhyn Chapter No. 159, as well as the local post office and library.

RAINBOW TAVERN ON U.S. 40   10 MILES WEST OF DONNER SUMMIT.

Many generations of Placer County families consider Rainbow Lodge in Soda Springs a beloved treasure. Originally, it was constructed as a stagecoach stop in 1869 for the busy area. The current lodge was erected in 1927, then expanded in 1930 using beams from nearby abandoned railroad sheds as part of its construction. It has seen several remodels through the years. The site is on the South Fork of the Yuba River and is known for rainbow trout fishing.

FOOTHILL COMMUNITIES

There were two Penryn Railroad sites over the years with the first depot, c. 1870–1890, built on the southwest corner of English Colony Way and the railroad tracks. The second depot, shown here, stood on the northwest corner. The building is next to the Penryn Fruit Company, the first shipping house in Penryn, having incorporated on February 11, 1886. The depot was conveniently located near Griffith Quarry and across from several fruit packing sheds.

WATER IS GOLD

In this 1892 photograph, a water flume is being built near Secret Town, east of Colfax. Water flumes, ditches, and canals were built throughout Placer County's gold country for miners to have access to water at their mining sites. As the area grew, these same waterways were utilized for development and ultimately became Placer County's "new" gold. (Courtesy Placer County Water Agency.)

Placer was the first
county in California to
develop its own water
system. The Placer
County Water Agency
was established in 1957
to ensure an adequate
supply of water for
county residents. The
beautiful Ralston Dam
and Afterbay Reservoir
is 89 feet high at an
elevation of 1,189 feet.
It has a gross storage of
2,800 acre-feet with a
surface area of 84 acres.
Twenty-three miles of
tunnels are affiliated
with this reservoir.
(Both, courtesy Placer
County Water Agency.)

WATER IS GOLD

Flumes or water ditches require constant maintenance. In the early days, the ditch tender's job was to ensure that ditches remained clear of leaves and other debris and also to check for failures so that local flooding was avoided. Today, workers are equipped with pickup trucks instead of horses, and ditch cleaning is made easier as a result of lining these waterways with gunite. The time-honored title of "ditch tender" is sometimes still used. (Both, courtesy Placer County Water Agency.)

An early covered bridge spans the banks of the North Fork of the American River. It was replaced by the much taller Foresthill bridge erected in 1973. At 730 feet, it is the highest bridge in California. It was built in anticipation of the Auburn Dam reservoir that would have been created if the dam had been completed. Today, the bridge provides easy access to Foresthill, Todd's Valley, and destinations in the Foresthill Divide. (Both, courtesy Placer County Water Agency.)

The water treatment plant in Auburn is shown here in the 1960s. As Placer County's population continues on an upward course, additional demands for water services increasingly escalate. The county population nearly doubled from 1980 to 1994. Today, growth and development are keeping at a rapid pace, and the agency's vision and foresight ensure it is prepared for 21st century expansion. (Both, courtesy Placer County Water Agency.)

The Hell Hole Dam and Reservoir is located at an elevation of 4,630 feet on the Rubicon River. Before construction, an 80-year-old dam-building expert viewed the area from a helicopter and exclaimed, "I have worked on the building of a lot of dams and the Hell Hole site is one of the best locations I have ever seen." Its gross storage is 207,590 acre-feet, and it is the water source for the Oxbow Power Station. (Both, courtesy Placer County Water Agency.)

The French Meadows Reservoir is near the headwaters of the Middle Fork of the American River and is a popular fishing and recreation area. At the time of its groundbreaking in June 1963, the French Meadows Reservoir was praised as the strongest and boldest water development in the state. Its height is 231 feet at an elevation of 5,273 feet. Gross water storage is 134,993 acre-feet with a surface area of 1,253 acres. (Both, courtesy Placer County Water Agency.)

The Auburn Iron Works building was established in 1865 as a blacksmith shop. Today, it serves as a wood scrapping business. "We all live in a watershed" is the driving force for significant management agreements in Placer County. In this photograph, water agency employees work to replace an open canal with a pipe at this Auburn site at the corner of Elm and Lincoln Streets. (Past image, courtesy Placer County Water Agency.)

WATER IS GOLD

INDEX

Discover Thousands of Local History Books
Featuring Millions of Vintage Images

Arcadia Publishing, the leading local history publisher in the United States, is committed to making history accessible and meaningful through publishing books that celebrate and preserve the heritage of America's people and places.

Find more books like this at
www.arcadiapublishing.com

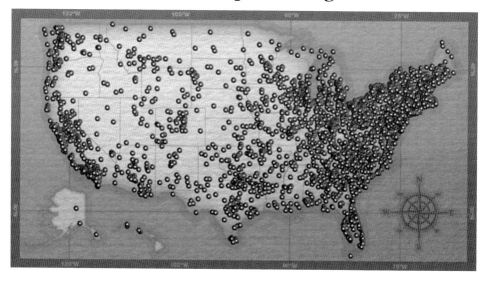

Search for your hometown history, your old stomping grounds, and even your favorite sports team.

Consistent with our mission to preserve history on a local level, this book was printed in South Carolina on American-made paper and manufactured entirely in the United States. Products carrying the accredited Forest Stewardship Council (FSC) label are printed on 100 percent FSC-certified paper.

MADE IN THE